DRIVEN TO SUCCEED

SCIENTISTS & INVENTORS WHO NEVER GAVE UP

BY
CHRIS SCHWAB

ILLUSTRATED BY
JOSHUA JANES

Rourke

Before Reading: *Building Background Knowledge and Vocabulary*

Building background knowledge can help children process new information and build upon what they already know. Before reading a book, it is important to tap into what children already know about the topic. This will help them develop their vocabulary and increase their reading comprehension.

Questions and Activities to Build Background Knowledge:

1. Look at the front cover of the book and read the title. What do you think this book will be about?
2. What do you already know about this topic?
3. Take a book walk and skim the pages. Look at the table of contents, photographs, captions, and bold words. Did these text features give you any information or predictions about what you will read in this book?

Vocabulary: *Vocabulary Is Key to Reading Comprehension*

Use the following directions to prompt a conversation about each word.

- Read the vocabulary words.
- What comes to mind when you see each word?
- What do you think each word means?

> **Vocabulary Words:**
> - *bankrupt*
> - *determination*
> - *invent*
> - *racism*
> - *resilient*
> - *visualized*

During Reading: *Reading for Meaning and Understanding*

To achieve deep comprehension of a book, children are encouraged to use close reading strategies. During reading, it is important to have children stop and make connections. These connections result in deeper analysis and understanding of a book.

Close Reading a Text

During reading, have children stop and talk about the following:

- Any confusing parts
- Any unknown words
- Text to text, text to self, text to world connections
- The main idea in each chapter or heading

Encourage children to use context clues to determine the meaning of any unknown words. These strategies will help children learn to analyze the text more thoroughly as they read.

When you are finished reading this book, turn to the next-to-last page for After-Reading Questions and an Activity.

Table of Contents

SUCCESS

Perseverance Pays Off ↑

Perseverance is something strong inside that helps you keep going no matter what. You *will* succeed—you just haven't yet!

Because someone persevered, we have light bulbs, smartphones, video games, umbrellas, 3D printers, and so much more.

"Enjoy failure and learn from it. You can never learn from success."
Sir James Dyson, inventor

TRY FAIL SUCCESS

Inventor SIR JAMES DYSON wasn't a quitter. To him, problems were something to solve. When he didn't like how vacuum cleaner bags clogged up and stopped working, he set out to **invent** a bagless vacuum cleaner to fix this problem.

Dyson's first bagless vacuum model flopped. So did the second one. Over the next five years, Dyson tested 5,126 bagless vacuum cleaner models. They all failed.

"We must have perseverance and, above all, confidence in ourselves."
Marie Curie, scientist

CYCLONE TECHNOLOGY

Determined to succeed, he kept trying. Finally, in 1982, model number 5,127 was a success! Today, Dyson machines are sold in 65 countries around the world.

THOMAS EDISON

TRY, TRY AGAIN

Inventor Thomas Edison may hold the record for the most trial runs before achieving success. It took him 10,000 tries to successfully invent the light bulb.

UNITED STATES POSTAGE
1879 FIRST EDISON'S LAMP 1929
ELECTRIC LIGHT'S
GOLDEN JUBILEE
2 CENTS 2

When Cuban scientist CARLOS JUAN FINLAY suggested in 1886 that the deadly disease yellow fever was spread by tiny mosquitoes, he was laughed at. People called him a "crazy old man."

But he didn't give up trying to convince people he was right. He continued investigating. He persevered!

CARLOS JUAN FINLAY

"Nothing in this world can take the place of persistence."
Calvin Coolidge, 30th US president

The disease continued to kill thousands of people for the next 20 years. Finlay kept on hatching mosquito eggs and testing volunteers to prove his theory. Finally, in 1900, experts agreed with Finlay's research, and they began controlling mosquitoes. Six years later, the yellow fever epidemic was over.

ACCIDENTAL ICE-CREAM CONES

When an ice-cream vendor at the 1904 St. Louis World's Fair ran out of paper cups for his ice cream, a nearby waffle seller came to the rescue. They joined forces and created the ice-cream cone.

ORVILLE AND WILBUR WRIGHT started out building and selling bicycles, but they dreamed of building bigger things—airplanes. So, in the early 1900s, the brothers started experimenting with gliders in Kitty Hawk, North Carolina.

WILBUR WRIGHT
OCTOBER 24, 1902

WRIGHT BROTHERS' BICYCLE

"Success is 99 percent failure."
Soichiro Honda, inventor

After more than 700 glider test flights, the furthest they had traveled was 622 feet (190 meters). They were disappointed with this. But instead of giving up, they **visualized** a better flying machine.

ORVILLE WRIGHT

WILBUR WRIGHT

visualized (VIZH-oo-uh-lized): saw a mental image

The Wright brothers' new flying machine used a small gasoline-powered engine and propellers. On its first flight, the engine stalled after three seconds and one of the propellers broke.

The Wrights persevered. They made changes. Weeks later, on December 17, 1903, their first successful engine-powered airplane flew for 59 seconds and landed 852 feet (37 meters) away. The first heavier-than-air flying machine was born!

"Failure is simply the opportunity to begin again, this time more intelligently."
   Henry Ford, inventor

HEAVIER-THAN-AIR HUMAN FLIGHT
DECEMBER 17, 1903

ACCIDENTAL BUBBLE WRAP™

Alfred Fielding and Marc Chavannes fed two shower curtains into a heat machine to make designer wallpaper. But when the sheets came out full of air bubbles, they had created something else instead—Bubble Wrap!

Tenacity Takes Over ↑

People with tenacity have the **determination** to succeed. They are tough inside and work toward their goals despite setbacks. They keep going!

"Let me tell you the secret that has led me to my goal. My strength lies solely in my tenacity."

Louis Pasteur, scientist

14

As a young Irish girl in the 1950s, everyone expected JOCELYN BELL BURNELL to take cooking classes. But she dreamt of becoming an astronomer, so her parents made sure she was allowed to take science classes. Classmates made fun of her for being the only girl in her honors science class.

JOCELYN BELL BURNELL

determination (di-tur-muh-NAY-shuhn): a strong will to do something

But, Burnell was tenacious. She continued studying astronomy and eventually became an astronomer. As a scientist, she helped build a radio telescope and read the data it picked up from the skies. One day in 1967, she noticed blinking signals in the data. Her boss called it a mistake, but she knew it wasn't.

"Remember to look up at the stars and not down at your feet."
Stephen Hawking, physicist

Burnell had discovered pulsars, the spinning cores of dying stars. A Nobel Prize was awarded for this important discovery, but it wasn't given to her. It was given to her boss! She was overlooked, most likely because she was a woman. But her tenacious personality helped her continue on with the career she loved.

JOCELYN BELL BURNELL

BETTER LATE THAN NEVER

Burnell finally received the credit she deserved. She was awarded the $3 million Breakthrough Prize, which she donated to help women and minorities study physics.

GARRETT
MORGAN

As a Black inventor in the South in the 1910s, GARRETT MORGAN encountered **racism**. Some people cared more about the color of his skin than about his inventions. But that didn't stop him.

After a factory fire killed 146 workers in 1911, Morgan invented a gas mask to help save people in smoke-filled emergencies. But because he was Black, no one wanted to buy his invention. He found a way around that.

NEW YORK
MARCH 25, 1911
FACTORY
FIRE

MEYERS
CROWN
&
WALLACH
CLOTHING

racism (RAY-sis-m): the systemic oppression of a racial group to the social, economic, and political advantage of another

Morgan hired a White actor to pose as the inventor and sell them while he demonstrated how they worked. He would put on a mask, go into a smoke-filled tent for up to 20 minutes ... and come out alive! His plan worked!

G. A. Morgan.
Breathing Device.

Application Filed
Aug. 19, 1912.

Fig. 2

Patented Oct. 13, 1914.

1,113,675.

a

c

f

b

d

e

Safety
Hood

Over 500 cities bought thousands of his Morgan Safety Hoods for their workers. The United States Army and Navy used them to protect soldiers. Morgan's creative thinking and tenacious personality saved countless lives around the world.

Exit 64 right

80

700 m

20:06

GLADYS WEST

GLADYS WEST

As a young Black girl in the South in the mid-1900s, Gladys West knew she would probably have to work in a factory or field. But she was determined to do something with her love of math. Overcoming her odds, she became a mathematician and helped invent the Global Positioning System (GPS).

Rebound with Resilience ↑

Resilient people are like rubber balls—they bounce back. No matter how many setbacks they experience, they rebound and try again. To them, failure is a learning opportunity.

"It's not how far you fall, but how high you bounce that counts."

Zig Ziglar, motivational speaker

MILTON HERSHEY knew he wanted to be a candymaker when he was a young boy. But, like many other inventors, he encountered setbacks before he tasted his sweet success. For him, the third time was a charm.

resilient (rih-ZIL-yuhnt): tending to recover from or adjust easily to misfortune or change

HERSHEY

Model industrial town and noted tourism destination established in 1903 and named for its founder, Milton S. Hershey (1857-1945). Hershey's companies developed housing, recreation, education, and cultural facilities, financial institutions, public utilities, a transit system, and the world's largest chocolate factory that opened in June, 1905.

PENNSYLVANIA HISTORICAL AND MUSEUM COMMISSION   2003

MILTON HERSHEY

In 1876, Hershey started his first candy business. It went **bankrupt**. His second candy business in 1883 went bankrupt too. On his third try, he found success with chewy caramels. He began by selling them door-to-door from a wooden pushcart. In 1886, he opened the Lancaster Caramel Company in Pennsylvania. It was a huge success.

"Never be limited by other people's limited imaginations."
**Mae C. Jemison,
NASA astronaut**

After years of selling caramels, Hershey became interested in something new—chocolate. It took him a few years, but he perfected the recipe for the Hershey chocolate bar right in his kitchen. He started selling them in 1900, some for just two cents each! Then, he created Hershey Kisses and started selling them in 1907. Hershey's resilience was a recipe for success.

SCIENCE CATCHES UP

Scientist EUNICE FOOTE, who first discovered the greenhouse effect and its link to global warming in 1856, did not receive credit for her discovery because she was a woman. But today, climate scientists celebrate her and her work.

bankrupt (BANK-rupt): unable to pay one's debts

MADAM C.J. WALKER was just seven years old when both of her parents died. As an orphan, she worked in the cotton fields of Mississippi, but the hard labor took a toll on her health. Little did she know that she would turn this misfortune into a real fortune in a few short years.

"Don't sit down and wait for the opportunities to come. Get up and make them."
**Madam C.J. Walker,
entrepreneur**

Madam C.J. Walker
Preparations
If you want Beauty of Complexion and loveliness of Hair, try Mme C.J.Walker's World Renowned Toilet Preparation.
(FULL DIRECTIONS ON EVERY BOTTLE.)

As a young woman, Walker's poor health led to hair loss. Hoping to help herself and other Black women with hair loss, she experimented at home with creating a secret formula for hair growth. One formula worked! Her hair grew back, and she was in business!

MADAM C.J. WALKER

33 USA

Slinky Craze Begins 1945

ACCIDENTAL SLINKY®

Naval engineer Richard James set out to design a large spring for ships. When one fell off the counter . . . it bounced over, under, over, under. He and his wife Betty thought it would make a great toy!

With just $1.25 to her name, Walker started selling her hair care products called "Madam Walker's Wonderful Hair Grower." First, she sold her hair products door-to-door. As her business grew, she sold them by mail. She eventually opened Walker Manufacturing Company and was able to give good, paying jobs to thousands of Black men and women.

"It is the courage to continue that counts."
Winston S. Churchill, British Prime Minister

As a resilient and inventive businesswoman, Madam C.J. Walker became one of the wealthiest Black women in America. She donated much of her wealth to African American charities and schools.

"If you haven't failed yet, you haven't tried anything."
Reshma Saujani,
Founder of *Girls Who Code*

OUT OF THE ASHES

Japanese inventor Akio Morita, one of the genius minds behind the Sony Corporation, had a few early ideas that flopped. His rice cooker burned rice, and his first tape recorder sounded horrible.

Memory Game

Look at the pictures. Can you retell their stories?

Index

After-Reading Questions

1. What did these scientists or inventors have in common?

2. Which person do you admire most? Give two reasons why.

3. How would the world be different if the Wright brothers had given up?

4. What does the author mean when she says, "Hershey's resilience was a recipe for success"?

5. Tell a friend about a time you showed perseverance, tenacity, or resilience.

Activity

Create a collage on a half-sheet of poster board. Cut out or draw pictures and words that show perseverance, tenacity, and resilience. These could be pictures of anyone who has worked hard to meet a goal, such as a sports figure or graduating student. Include word labels that describe these qualities such as *determination* or *hard work*.

About the Author

Chris Schwab is a former teacher and writer currently living in Greensboro, North Carolina. Her life's dream since a child was to become an author. She read books, wrote lots of stories, and took writing classes. She persevered and now has the pleasure of creating books for a living.

About the Illustrator

Joshua Janes' love of drawing and his family's support lent him the resilience, tenacity, and perseverance needed to obtain a career as an illustrator from his studio in Ohio.

www.rourkebooks.com

PHOTO CREDITS ©: cover: Yoshio Tsunoda/AFLO/Newscom; cover: Dennis Brack / DanitaDelimont.com; cover: scanrail/GettyImages; cover: lucentius/GettyImages; cover: Madam C.J. Walker Manufacturing/Heritage Art/Heritage Images AiWire/Newscom; cover: Ben-Ari/Avalon/Newscom; cover: Cem Ekiztas/Shutterstock; cover: New Africa/Shutterstock; pg all: Aleksandr Artt/Shutterstock; pg all: Paladin12/Shutterstock; pg all: robbin lee/Shutterstock; pg all: Rtstudio/Shutterstock; pg 1: Rafael Ben-Ari/Avalon/Newscom; pg 1: Flas100/Shutterstock; pg 3: Richard B. Levine/Newscom; pg 3: ESB Professional/Shutterstock; pg 3: Carlos E. Santa Maria/Shutterstock; pg 4: VladimirFLoyd/GettyImages; pg 4: ESB Professional/Shutterstock; pg 4: Carlos E. Santa Maria/Shutterstock; pg 4: faithie/Shutterstock; pg 5: Floortje/GettyImages; pg 5: Electric Egg/Shutterstock; pg 5: Flas100/Shutterstock; pg 6: TSV-art/Shutterstock; pg 6: Papin Lab/Shutterstock; pg 6: NICK VEASEY/SCIENCE PHOTO LIBRARY/Newscom; pg 7: Michael Rega/Shutterstock; pg 7: Everett Collection/Shutterstock; pg 7: picoStudio/Shutterstock; pg 7: ECO LENS/Shutterstock; pg 7: Glen Stubbe/ZUMA Press/Newscom; pg 8: Everett Collection/Newscom; pg 8: blackred/GettyImages; pg 8: nechaev-kon/GettyImages; pg 9: picoStudio/Shutterstock; pg 9: artjazz/Shutterstock; pg 10: Edwin Remsberg / VWPics/Newscom; pg 10: Everett Collection/Shutterstock; pg 11: Dennis Brack / DanitaDelimont.com / "Danita Delimont Photography"/Newscom; pg: 11: ESB Professional/Shutterstock; pg 11: Flas100/Shutterstock; pg 11: Library Of Congress/ZUMA Press/Newscom; pg 11: Library Of Congress/ZUMA Press/Newscom; pg 12: traveler1116/GettyImages; pg 13: Wavebreakmedia/GettyImages; pg 13: picoStudio/Shutterstock; pg 13: Hilary Jane Morgan/ZUMA Press/Newscom; pg 14: bubaone/GettyImages; pg 14: GoodIdeas/Shutterstock; pg 15: Flas100/Shutterstock; pg 15: Maria_Domnikova/Shutterstock; pg 15: Cover Images/ZUMAPRESS/Newscom; pg 16: zhengzaishuru/Shutterstock; pg 16: AstroStar/Shutterstock; pg 17: picoStudio/Shutterstock; pg 17: DA5/Drew Altizer/WENN/Newscom; pg 18: ASSOCIATED PRESS; pg 19: blackred/GettyImages; pg 19: EKramar/GettyImages; pg 19: Flas100/Shutterstock; pg 19: UPI/Newscom; pg 19: UPI/Newscom; pg 20: ESB Professional/Shutterstock; pg 21: Adrian Cadiz; pg 21: Steppeua/GettyImages; pg 21: Pincasso/Shutterstock; pg 21: picoStudio/Shutterstock; pg 22: Audio und werbung/Shutterstock; pg 22: Twinsterphoto/Shutterstock; pg 22: travelershigh/Shutterstock; pg 22: Savvapanf Photo/Shutterstock; pg 23: Everett Collection/Newscom; pg 23: George Sheldon/Shutterstock; pg 23: Flas100/Shutterstock; pg 23: Lissandra Melo/Shutterstock; pg 23: George Sheldon/Shutterstock; pg 23: Amy Lutz/Shutterstock; pg 25: picoStudio/Shutterstock; pg 25: Ed Connor/Shutterstock; pg 25: Flas100/Shutterstock; pg 26: Everett Collection/Newscom; pg 26: Everett Collection/Newscom; pg 26: blackred/GettyImages; pg 26: EKramar/GettyImages; pg 27: David Joles/ZUMA Press/Newscom; pg 27: picoStudio/Shutterstock; pg 27: MM_photos/Shutterstock; pg 28: Unknown/Heritage Art/Heritage Images AiWire/Newscom; pg 28: Madam C.J. Walker Manufacturing/Heritage Art/Heritage Images AiWire/Newscom; pg 29: Yoshio Tsunoda/AFLO/Newscom; pg 29: sunstock/GettyImages; pg 29: picoStudio/Shutterstock

QUOTE SOURCES: pg 4: brainyquote.com; pg 6: mariecurie.org.uk; pg 8: growthink.com; pg 10: brainyquote.com; pg 12: eatwell101.com; pg 14: quoteinvestigator.com; pg 16: nytimes.com; pg 22: goodreads.com; pg 24: goodreads.com; pg 26: brainyquote.com; pg 28: graciousquotes.com

Edited by: Catherine Malaski   Cover & interior design/illustration by: Joshua Janes

Library of Congress PCN Data

Scientists & Inventors Who Never Gave Up / Chris Schwab
(Driven to Succeed)
ISBN 978-1-73165-769-5 (hard cover) (alk. paper)
ISBN 978-1-73165-781-7 (e-book)
ISBN 978-1-73165-779-4 (soft cover)
ISBN 978-1-73165-783-1 (e-pub)
Library of Congress Control Number: 2023941672

Rourke Educational Media
Printed in the United States of America
01-0152411937